God Told Me To Tell You...

Winifred Smith Eure

To order additional copies of this book, contact:
Xlibris
1-888-795-4274
www.Xlibris.com
Orders@Xlibris.com

ISBN: Softcover   978-1-9845-7835-8
        EBook   978-1-9845-7834-1

Print information available on the last page

Rev. date: 06/12/2020

DEDICATION

This book is dedicated to the memory of all my loved ones who have transitioned to be with the Lord: my husband, Clarence, for being a good partner; my parents, who sacrificed so much for me; my brothers, who helped to shape my life's story; my aunts, uncles and cousins for great childhood memories of being together; and my in-laws for their faithfulness.

Contents

God Told Me To Tell You...

Introduction

I grew up in a house of boys and acquired a fondness for sports, board games and playing cards as they did. However, Sunday was a day when Mom's paramount influence emerged, and that was her taking us to Sunday School and to Heard AME Church.

I was all girl on Sundays, from head to toe. I remember getting my hair done, preparing the night before by choosing my dress with the crinoline slip, patent leather shoes and purse. And at least three times a year, I recited in the Sunday School Christmas, Easter, and Children's Day programs, always practicing and memorizing my part and learning how to curtsy.

Mr. Jenkins and his wife are among the early church leaders who I vaguely remember. As a teenager I sang in the youth choir, ushered, and was a member of the YPD when my mom was one of the supervisors. Mrs. Eunice Marrow, who later became Sunday School Superintendent, was famous for teaching catechism and staging spelling bees. She appeared to be very serious-minded and strict.

Reverend Kelsey and Reverend Gipson were pastors who I was fond of, but Rev. T. R. Goyins was my favorite. What a nice man! When I later became a Newark teacher, he kindly accepted my invitation to visit my classroom on Community Leaders Day, speaking to and encouraging my students to be the best they could be. It was under his influence that I truly learned what it meant to be a Christian in my heart, not the outside trimmings. He counseled and married my husband, Clarence, and me.

I love Heard African Methodist Episcopal Church! And I attribute that mostly to my mother, who was a member until she made her transition to be with the Lord in 1997. Also, because I think of Heard as a body of believers who are trying to live right, which includes helping others. Our current pastor, Rev. Stephen A. Green (who is so humble and, at the same time, an educated man), has inspired change and an embracing of this technological age we find ourselves in, accommodating all generations at Heard. His ministry is all about experiencing God not only on Sunday but every day.

This book of poems is essentially an outpouring of my spirit, my faith, my joy, and my desire to share my innermost thoughts about our Heavenly Father (via freestyle and some storytelling) with those of you who believe in Jesus Christ, the Son of God; that he was crucified, buried, and resurrected on the third day; and that he is coming again.

"Whatever my lot, Thou has taught me to say "It is well, it is well with my soul."

The Presence of Jesus' Love

You can be happy.
You can have love.
The heart and deeds
Of a loved one sent from above.

You can be happy.
You can have joy.
The miracle birth
Of a girl or boy.

You can be happy.
You can discover your gifts
To share with others
Encourage and uplift.

You can be happy.
You can have peace
A mind and soul of wisdom
That with God's will won't cease.

You can be happy.
You can have friends
To talk, travel, play with
Days, months, and years on end.

You can be happy.
You can know Jesus.
He is closer than a brother
And is forever with us.

You can be happy
With everything from above.
For all things are possible
In the presence of Jesus' love.

The Word of God

Is powerful and rich.
The likeness of which
there is none; undeniably true
and refreshingly new
to someone to whom it is preached.
God is calling you and calling me.
The time is ripe.
Be revived again in this season
for there is still reason
to be saved.

Cling to his promises.
Yield to his throne.
Go forward in faith.
Never alone.

The Word of God
is authentic and fruitful.
For the elderly and youthful.
It is sharp and clean.
God is calling you and calling me.
He is waiting today for your hand
and your heart to receive his love
and to do your part on this earth.
Sing his praises. Be clothed in his
armor. Pray without ceasing.

Spread the Word of the Father.
The Great I Am
Jesus Christ
is coming again!

A Mother's Love

One night I lay awake
with a lot on my mind.
I thought of my children
and wanted to be kind.

How could I best show them
the love that I feel?
Ease their troubles
and help them to heal?

I cried a tear
Maybe two or three.
I knelt near my bed
and on my knee.

I prayed for the answers
that would comfort and free them.
I prayed for their spiritual growth
and redeeming.

Then made a phone call
to each one separately.
And reassured them
In their corner, I will be.

But entrusted to all
the gift of Jesus Christ.
And encouraged them
to keep him close in their life.

God's Rest

Have you entered God's rest?
Are you reassured
he'll take care of you?
Have you understood

That above all fact
and circumstance
he is ultimate love—
more than a first chance?

He'll order your steps.
Multiply your faith.
Doesn't mean that you're dying.
Just want to seek his face.

The Holy Spirit
that inner Light
gives purpose and peace
the gift of spiritual insight.

Have you entered God's rest?
Do you feel his embrace?
Are you certain without doubt
in this holy place?

Watch and wait!
Kneel and pray!
Be grateful
when Jesus has his way.

When I Grow Up

Grandma asked me
what I want to be
when I grow up.

I replied, Grandma, I don't know.
Gonna go with the flow
right now.

She sat me down
and gave me some sound
advice.

You are at the age where you need some
direction.
So start your reflection
of the things you can do and need do better;

Of your heart's will to serve
and to get up the nerve
to acquire knowledge

And skill to
a path that will fulfill
your innermost dream and God's will.

Then ask God to guide
you and dare Satan to hide
this from you.

Get help from your teachers
your parents
your preacher.

Start to prepare now.
If you change your mind—Wow!
You're human.

The future doesn't have to look grim.
Just don't settle for a whim.
Let your light shine!

God Told Me To Tell You...

Something Within

There is something deep within
That is stronger than
A mighty wind.

There is something deep within
That comforts me
Through thick and thin.

There is something deep within
That gives me grace
To resist sin.

There is something deep within
That keeps me connected
To friends and kin.

There is something deep within
That chooses my battles
And lets love win.

There is something deep within
That directs my pathways
For where and when.

There is something deep within
That kindles my faith
Again and again.

There is something deep within
That keeps a song in my heart
A heavenly hymn.

There is something deep within
That guides me
To his word often.

That something is the rock on which I stand
My Lord and Savior Jesus
With him I speak, "I can."

God Is in Control

(Whatever Your Cross)

It was after midnight.
She stood pacing the floor
wondering what all
this heartache was for.

Two days ago
she'd been diagnosed with cancer.
Her mind told her now
that God was the answer.

She got on her knees
And prayed a sweet prayer.
The voice of an angel
was heard in the air.

Daughter you're older now
and in need of more rest.
Your Father in heaven
says you have been blessed.

Though Satan may send you
one of his arrows,
keep walking in light
the straight and the narrow.

Should God call you home
his need of you more,
he'll walk you safely and peacefully
through his heavenly door.

There's no need to fret.
No need of regret.
The Savior has
his hands on you yet.

That Precious Place

Steal away
To that precious place
Where on bended knees
You seek God's face.

Where you speak to him
So humbly, so true
Asking for his mercy
And his saving grace too.

The Savior
Knows your heart and soul.
Confess your sins
Let him make you whole.

Yield your all
To his guide and lead.
Submit to his will
In word and deed.

No love
Greater than his on earth.
Be born again.
For this second birth

Gives light and joy
And peace to all
Who abide in him
And heed his call

To be Christian like
In all you do.
Share the gospel with family
Friends and strangers too

Of Jesus' birth and atoning death
His sacrifice for humankind
His resurrection—
A gift for all times.

Yes, steal away to Jesus.
Set you inner voice free.
Reveal to him your true self.
See how faithful he will be.

Steal away!

Women's Day

Hallelujah!

It's Women's Day.
Another day
the Lord has made.
He is the "Truth, the Life, the Way."

We hear the Word.
We kneel to pray.
We fellowship.
We are God's clay

To mold and fashion
by his will.
We grant God glory.
We honor him still.

We give tithes and
offerings.
Especially grateful
for all things.

We dine
with family and friends.
We cherish each moment
from beginning to end.

Hallelujah!
It's Women's Day.
We claim our history.
In church we will stay.

There's much work
that needs be done.
There's many blessings
to be won.

And those who have
transitioned to heaven above
we are thankful for
their legacy of love.

HAPPY WOMEN'S DAY

I've Told My Story

I've told my story
And I'm runnin' my race.
I won't look back
And I won't lose face.

Got a friend in Jesus.
Got some sista friends too.
Got a heart of joy.
Daily troubles few.

Prayin' and trustin' in faith
Like a child of God ought.
Heedin' his will for my life.
Abidin' in truths he taught.

Gonna enjoy my days.
And hope for peace during the night.
Gonna celebrate my freedom.
Gonna shine my light.

Love my family.
Wanna love my foes.
Gonna stand for something.
Have some seeds to sow.

Not afraid of dyin'.
Not afraid of life.
Not afraid of choosin'
To "walk by faith, not by sight."

Author

Printed in the United States
By Bookmasters